Take your camera to FRANCE

Ted Park

Raintree

www.raintreepublishers.co.uk

Visit our website to find out more information about Raintree books.

To order:

☎ Phone 44 (0) 1865 888112

🖹 Send a fax to 44 (0) 1865 314091

🖥 Visit the Raintree Bookshop at www.raintreepublishers.co.uk to browse our catalogue and order online

First published in Great Britain by Raintree Publishers, Halley Court, Jordan Hill, Oxford OX2 8EJ, part of Harcourt Education. Raintree is a registered trademark of Harcourt Education Ltd.

© Harcourt Education Ltd 2003
First published in paperback in 2004
The moral right of the proprietor has been asserted.

Produced for Raintree by Discovery Books
Editors: Isabel Thomas and Gianna Williams
Cover design: Jo Sapwell (www.tipani.co.uk)

Printed and bound in China by South China Printing Company

ISBN 1 844 21187 8 (hardback)
07 06 05 04 03
10 9 8 7 6 5 4 3 2 1

ISBN 1 844 21195 9 (paperback)
08 07 06 05 04
10 9 8 7 6 5 4 3 2 1

British Library cataloguing in Publication Data
Park, Ted
France. – (Take Your Camera to)
523.8

A full catalogue record for this book is available from the British Library.

Acknowledgements
The publishers would like to thank the following for permission to reproduce photographs: p.**i** Jean Kugler/FPG International; p.**3** (Eiffel Tower) CORBIS; p.**3** (boy) Arthur Tilley/FPG International; p.**3** (girl) Corel; p.**4** Chris Salvo/FPG International; p.**7** (both) Cartesia Software; pp.**8, 9** Telegraph Colour Library/FPG International; p.**10** CORBIS; p.**11** Telegraph Colour Library/FPG International; p.**13** Tom Craig/FPG International; p.**15** (both) Corel; p.**17** (castle) Jean Kugler/FPG International; p.**17** (train) Telegraph Colour Library/FPG International; p.**19** Vladimir Pcholkin/FPG International; p.**23** Rex Features; p.**25** Arthur Tilley/FPG International; p.**27** Stephen Simpson/FPG International; p.**28** (Paris) Telegraph Colour Library/FPG International; p.**29** (beach) Telegraph Colour Library/FPG International; p.**29** (map) Cartesia Software. Additional photos PhotoDisc.

Cover photograph of the Eiffel Tower reproduced with permission of Stock Photos/Corbis.

All statistics in the Quick Facts section come from The New York Times Almanac (2002) and The World Almanac (2002).

Every effort has been made to contact copyright holders of any material reproduced in this book. Any omissions will be rectified in subsequent printings if notice is given to the publishers.

Contents

This is France 4

The place 6

Paris 10

Places to visit 12

The people 14

Life in France 16

Government and religion 18

Earning a living 20

Schools and sport 22

Food and festivals 24

The future 26

Quick facts about France 28

Glossary 30

Index 32

Any words appearing in the text in bold, **like this**, are explained in the glossary.

This is France

France is a large country in north-western Europe. It has tall mountains, grassy plains and sandy beaches. If you took your camera to France, you could take photographs of many things.

France has many interesting cities, like Paris, the country's capital. Paris has many famous sights that you can photograph, like the **Eiffel Tower** and the **Arc de Triomphe**.

The Arc de Triomphe is a well-known sight in Paris.

In the countryside, you might see grapevines being pruned.

France also has beautiful countryside, dotted with small farms. You might see vineyards there, where grapes are grown and places where some of France's famous cheeses are made.

This book will show you some of these places. It will also tell you much about the country of France. When you take your camera to France, you will enjoy your visit more.

The place

France is the second-largest country in Europe. It is about 805 kilometres (500 miles) from north to south and the same from east to west. This is more than twice the size of the United Kingdom.

Much of France borders the sea. To the north is the English Channel. The Atlantic Ocean is to the west, while to the south is the Mediterranean Sea.

Along part of the southern coast of France is an area called the Riviera. There are many sandy beaches and holiday resorts there.

France has a varied landscape. Much of France is made up of grassy plains, where farming is the main occupation. Forests cover about a quarter of the country. France has lots of rivers, and the canals that join many of them make it easy for boats to sail from one part of the country to another.

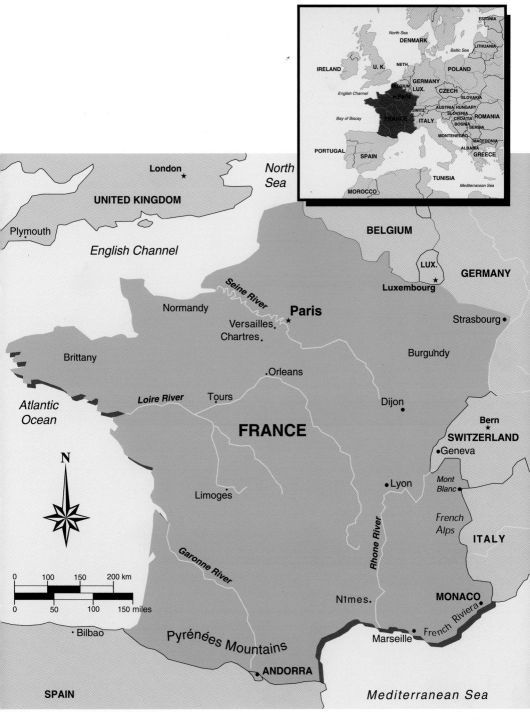

ESTONIA
North Sea
DENMARK
Baltic Sea
LITHUANIA
IRELAND
U. K.
NETH.
POLAND
GERMANY
BELGIUM
LUX.
CZECH
SLOVAKIA
English Channel
Paris
AUSTRIA HUNGARY
SWITZ.
SLOVENIA
ROMANIA
FRANCE
CROATIA
BOSNIA
Bay of Biscay
ITALY
SERBIA
MONTENEGRO
MACEDONIA
ALBANIA
GREECE
PORTUGAL
SPAIN
TUNISIA
Mediterranean Sea
MOROCCO

London ★
North Sea

UNITED KINGDOM

BELGIUM

Plymouth

English Channel

LUX.
Luxembourg ★

GERMANY

Seine River

Normandy

Paris ★

Strasbourg •

Versailles •
Chartres •

Burgundy

• Orleans

Brittany

Loire River
Tours

Dijon •

Bern ★
SWITZERLAND

Atlantic
Ocean

FRANCE

• Geneva

N

Limoges •

• Lyon

Mont
Blanc •

French
Alps

ITALY

| 0 | 100 | 150 | 200 km |

Garonne River

MONACO

| 0 | 50 | 100 | 150 miles |

N1mes •

French Riviera •

• Bilbao

Pyrénées Mountains

Marseille •

ANDORRA

SPAIN

Mediterranean Sea

7

France has many mountains, too. The Pyrénées mountains in the south divide France and Spain. In the east are the French Alps, with some of Europe's tallest peaks. The highest of these is Mont Blanc, at about 4807 metres high.

The high peaks in the French Alps are a beautiful sight.

Much of France has a temperate climate. This means that in most places it is fairly mild for most of the year. However, the mountains are snow-capped for much of the year. Along the Mediterranean coast, it is hot almost all the time.

The French Riviera is a popular holiday destination. You could take a picture of one of its sandy beaches.

Paris

The capital of France is one of the best-known cities in the world. Many people come here from all over the world. Paris is full of wide streets, green parks and old buildings.

   One of the most famous sights is the **Eiffel Tower**, opened in 1889. Visitors can take the lift to the top.

The Eiffel Tower is one of the most popular places in Paris for tourists to visit. It is 300 metres tall.

The Grande Arche de la Défense is a spectacular sight.

Paris has many museums and art galleries. The most famous is the Louvre. Hundreds of people go there every day to see its many works of art.

If you take your camera on the streets of Paris, you can photograph all sorts of sights, like the **Arc de Triomphe**. This grand arch is at one end of a wide street called the Champs-Elysées. The arch was built in 1836. Further down is another arch. It is known as the Grande Arche de la Défense. This arch was opened in 1989. These two arches show how old and new are found side by side in Paris.

Places to visit

In ancient times, France was a **colony** of the Roman Empire, known as Gaul. The Romans built many things while they were in France. One of the most famous is an aqueduct in Nîmes, a city in southern France. An aqueduct carries water to places where it is needed.

A favourite place to visit in Paris is Nôtre Dame. This famous **cathedral** took almost 200 years to build and can seat more than 6000 people. Visitors can climb to the top of Nôtre Dame to take photographs of the city of Paris.

Louis XIV (14th) was a king of France. He ruled from 1643 to 1715. During his time as king, he lived in a beautiful palace at Versailles. The palace is about 24 kilometres (15 miles) from Paris. It is famous for its 'hall of mirrors' and its gardens.

The gardens of Versailles are known for their fountains.

The people

There are almost 60 million people living in France and they come from many different backgrounds. Viking invaders from Scandinavia came to the region of Normandy in northern France over 1000 years ago. The people who live in Brittany, in the north-west corner of the country, are called Bretons. These people speak a **Celtic** language that is similar to Welsh or Cornish. The **Basque** people who live in the Pyrénées also speak a language that is quite different to French.

France has many **immigrants**. They have moved from other countries to make their homes in France. Some of these immigrants are from places that France once ruled, like Vietnam, Algeria, Tunisia and Morocco. The immigrants bring their cooking styles and customs with them. These different people make France a very interesting country.

A Parisian, with his lunch of bread and cheese.

This young girl is from Burgundy, a region in the east of France.

15

Life in France

People in different parts of France have very different lifestyles. Many French people have left the countryside to live in the towns and cities, but they remain very loyal to their home region. Even city dwellers often keep a small home in the country where they can relax at weekends and holiday times.

For many French people, family life is very important. French workers get about six weeks' holiday each year and like to spend their holidays with their families.

Some families may visit other countries for their holidays but many like to travel in France, especially to the south of the country, which has long, hot summers. Travelling around France is easy because the country has good roads and fast, efficient trains. The fastest trains are known as TGV, which stands for *Train à Grande Vitesse*. In English, this means 'fast train'.

The French
countryside
has many old
châteaux.
They make
very good
photographs.

One of
France's fast
trains, known
as TGV, races
through
France. It will
take you to
many places
quickly.

17

Government and religion

France has been a republic since 1789. This means that the leader, or president, is elected. Elections take place every seven years. Then the president appoints a prime minister who helps the president to run the country. There are two groups that make laws. They are the National Assembly and the Senate. The citizens of France elect people to these places.

Most French people are **Roman Catholics**, and French towns and villages nearly always have splendid churches and **cathedrals** at their centre. About 2 per cent of French people are **Protestants**. France also has about four million **Muslims**. Many of these Muslims used to live in France's African **colonies**.

You can photograph many cathedrals in France. This is the cathedral and old town of Chartres.

18

Earning a living

Farming is a major **industry** in France because there is so much good farmland in the country. France is Europe's largest grower of wheat, barley and maize. Farms used to.be small, and the work was done by hand. Now machines do most of the work.

France is famous for its wine, and it makes more than any other country in the world. It is France's biggest **export**. This means that France ships more wine overseas than any other product. Most of the grapes used to make wine are grown in the east and the south.

Other important industries include space **technology** and the car, chemical and electrical industries. Aeroplane construction is also a growing business. The Airbus is fast becoming one of the world's most popular passenger aeroplanes, and it is built in France.

The French make fine perfumes and clothing. You can buy these products all over the world.

More than 52 million visitors come to France each year. It is important that they are treated well, so the service industry is very big. It provides many jobs in hotels, restaurants and transport.

**If you visit the grape-growing countryside,
you can photograph farm workers such as these.**

Schools and sport

Young people in France have to go to school from the age of six to sixteen. Then they may go on for two more years, until they are eighteen. During these two years, students go to schools called *lycées*.

Schoolchildren usually have a longer school day than those in the UK, and they may have to go to school on Saturday mornings, too. At eighteen, students may go on to university. The most famous of France's 102 universities is the Sorbonne, in Paris, which is around 800 years old.

Many French people enjoy sport. Cycling is a very popular sport in France. The annual Tour de France cycle race goes all over the country and takes about three weeks. Motor racing is another favourite French sport. The annual Le Mans race is famous because it lasts 24 hours. Football is the favourite team sport.

Races are exciting events to photograph. This is a photo of the Tour de France at the Arc de Triomphe in Paris.

food and festivals

The French love cooking and their food is world-famous. The favourite bread in France is a *baguette*, made in a long loaf. Croissants are rich rolls made of eggs, flour and butter. Baguettes and croissants are enjoyed in other parts of the world as well. Quiche is a French dish that has also become well known in many places. Quiche is a mixture of eggs, cream and cheese that is baked in a pie crust.

The most important holiday to the French is Bastille Day, on 14 July. This date marks the beginning of the French Revolution in 1789. On that day the poor people in Paris rose up against their king. The people attacked the Bastille, a prison in the centre of Paris. Today, on Bastille Day, there may be parties, parades and fireworks. If you visit France on Bastille Day, you can take photographs of the exciting things that happen on this day.

Most French people celebrate Easter and Christmas. Other festivals often honour what farmers grow in their particular region. Sometimes fruits, wines or cheeses are at the centre of these harvest festivals.

A young child carries home some baguettes.

The future

If you took your camera to France, you would see a country that is changing. France is at the centre of the European Union, a group of European countries that have joined together to improve trade and understanding. France has recently changed its currency from the franc to the euro.

The Channel Tunnel helps people travel from Paris to London quickly. It now takes just three hours to travel between these cities.

However, like other nations, France has some problems. In many **industries**, people's jobs are being replaced by high-tech machines. There are many cars on the roads of France that pollute the air. In the cities, there are the problems of unemployment and poverty.

The people of France want to solve these problems. They are proud of their country. As the French say, '*Vive la France*', which means 'Long live France.'

A modern glass pyramid stands in front of the Louvre in Paris.

Quick facts about
FRANCE

Capital
Paris

Borders
Belgium,
Luxembourg,
Germany, Monaco,
Switzerland, Italy, Spain.

Area
543,965 square kilometres
(210,024 square miles)

Population
60.5 million

Largest cities
Paris (10,952,011 people);
Lyon (1,406,043 people);
Lille (1,182,026 people)

Main crops
cereal grains, sugar beet, potatoes,
wine grapes

Natural resources
coal, iron ore, bauxite

Longest river
Loire, at 1020 km (634 miles)

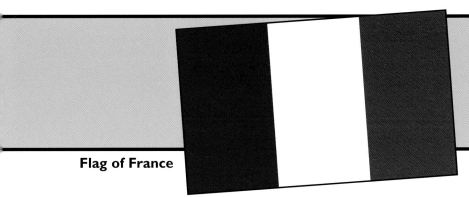

Flag of France

◄ **Coastline**
3428 km (2130 miles)

Monetary unit
euro

Literacy rate
99 per cent of French people can read and write.

Major industries
steel, machinery, chemicals, food products, tourism

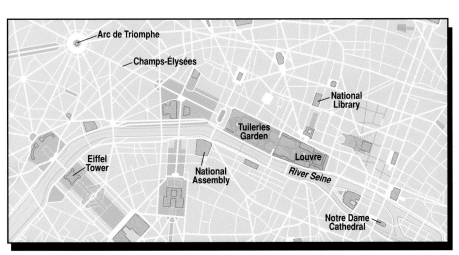

Map of Paris

29

Glossary

Arc de Triomphe (ark deh TREE-omf) triumphal arch in the centre of Paris built by Napoleon. It has become a symbol of national pride.

Basques (BASKS) people based in the Pyrenees Mountains, on the borders of Spain and France, whose language is unlike Spanish or French

cathedral main church of an area, where the bishop of that area is based

Celtic (KEL-tik) word describing a group of people who inhabited much of Europe in pre-Roman times. Parts of their languages still survive in modern-day Irish, Cornish and Welsh.

colony land that has been settled by people from another country

Eiffel Tower (EYE-fuhl) famous steel tower in Paris that was built to celebrate the scientific and engineering achievements of the 19th century. It was the tallest structure in the world until the Empire State Building was built 40 years later.

export when goods are sent out of a country